S T I L L

I

S T A N D

A MEMOIR

CHRISTAL STRANGE

Book Cover Design: Prize Publishing House

Printed by: Prize Publishing House, LLC in the United States of America.

First printing edition 2023.

Prize Publishing House
P.O. Box 9856, Chesapeake, VA 23321
www.PrizePublishingHouse.com

Library of Congress Control Number: 2023906347

ISBN (Paperback): 979-8-9875046-2-8
ISBN (E-Book): 979-8-9875046-3-5

CONTENTS

PRELUDE

I've been bullied, molested, and raped. I also allowed myself to feel worthless and not enough. I've been depressed. I've cried to die. Suicidal thoughts came more than once. Hey, but "Still, I Stand."

Through the many experiences I have had to live and learn through, most people do not know that I had my very first story copy written at fourteen. It is titled *Why Me*. This story was written from my experience of being bullied because I was skinny due to my heart condition. I spoke up for myself and my feelings, which yielded a good result. Tolerance and friendship conquered the fear of the unknown.

> *"My brethren, count it all joy when ye fall into divers temptations; Knowing this, that the trying of your faith worketh patience. But let patience have her perfect work, that ye may be perfect and entire, wanting nothing."*
> *~ James 1:2-4, KJV*

> *"But seek ye first the kingdom of God, and his righteousness; and all these things shall be added unto you."*
> *~ Matthew 6:33, KJV*

The strength that the Creator has given me is beyond anything the mind can wrap itself around and is beyond anything any person I've known has ever been able to give. Part of the glory of the salvation plan is that it allows us to access that loving advice as we spend time building our personal relationships with God, and the Holy Spirit begins guiding and directing our lives. We must remind ourselves that this means Jesus will be there for us through anything and beyond any expectation because He is the same every day. He never changes, and His promises can never be taken away.

We often know that we can't be completely removed from these experiences and that we might not reach perfect healing in our present lives. Still, since we can take comfort in knowing that God has a plan for each of our lives, it removes the fear of insecurity, just believing that He will keep doing as He always has. He will never put more on any person than He knows they can handle, and that is just the thing. We are shaped through our lives to be tempered like a sword. If you have ever watched someone smithing and creating swords, you know that they use both fire and ice to temper the blade. They put it through so many rounds of icing and burning. God tempers us through time and experience to make us stronger so that we will be a piercing blade and valuable in life. We can call upon our Father, as His children, at any time to uplift us and make us stronger. This is one of the beautiful blessings of having a close relationship with our Creator. At any given point, we just have to enter into prayer with God, and He will emerge to deliver us just as He has always done and promised to do.

DEDICATION

I want to dedicate this to my mother, who was there when it wasn't easy to show what love is all about. Also, to my brothers and my church family. Heavenly grandmas, Mildred and Ruth. Granddaddy Gersi, Uncle Tom, Uncle Roc, Lyreal, Cindy, James, Dwayne, my Auntie Sandra, songbird Rayven, Evangelist (Auntie) Michelle, Pastor and First Lady Grant.

Last but not least, my bestie Michelle.

Carolinas HealthCare System
Levine Children's Hospital

October 24th, 2013

To whom it may concern,

I am writing in regards to the support needed by Ms. Elaine Sylvia Wright during a very difficult time for her family. Christal Lakisha Strange, Ms. Wright's thirty-three year old daughter, was born with complex congenital heart disease and has undergone numerous open heart surgeries and catheter interventions over her life. During her recent pregnancy, Christal experienced profound congestive heart failure and was referred to me for surgical repair of two vales within her heart. I operated on Christal September 27, 2013. The operation was long and very complex.

Unfortunately, Christal suffered a devastating brain injury during her operation that has left her severely disabled.

Christal has two children in her custody (3 year old Madison Strange and 6 month old I'yanna Johnson). Christal's mother is very involved in Christal's life as a mother, grandmother, care giver and decision maker while Christal is in the hospital. Ms. Wright will most certainly be involved in the long term care of Christal and her grandchildren as Christal will be disabled the rest of her life. Ms. Wright, being the next of kin, will need all the services currently provided to the children and Christal to continue for an indefinite amount of time. Please provide Ms. Wright every opportunity available to allow for this transition during a very difficult time in her family's life. Should you require further information regarding this difficult situation, please do not hesitate to contact my office at 704-373-1813.

Sincerely,

Thomas S Maxey MD
Pediatric and Adult Congenital Cardiac
Surgery Levine Children's Hospital

INTRODUCTION

"For God so loved the world, that he gave his only begotten Son, that whosoever believeth in him should not perish, but have everlasting life."

~ JOHN 3:16, KJV

have come to know that I was destined to one day share my testimony with everyone willing to listen and the entire world. My struggles have made it possible for me to bring a unique message to others and be a major blessing as I show them the promised path of restoration and how they can experience the same abundance of miracles as I have.

Throughout my life, I have been incredibly blessed with many miracles from my conception until now. Just recently, however, I have felt compelled by God to share my experience with Him and to share my story.

Of all the things I have to share, the most important one is the miracle of salvation, which came when I chose to accept Jesus Christ as my Lord and Savior. The most important aspect of that miracle is knowing that our souls are the most valuable thing we have and that God thought of this when He created His perfect rescue plan. I feel that sharing this is the one gift that I will keep on giving to everyone who reads my story.

God has so much in store for all of us, and if we give Him a chance to develop a relationship, we can all sing His praises as we find ourselves free from the bondage of sin and the crushing weight of darkness that seems to thrive in the world around us.

I had to learn not to allow my trials to have victory over me and not to fall into my sinful ways again due to my impatience, anger, or momentary upsets. It's a lot easier to find things to be grateful for when you take the time to account for your blessings rather than continually focusing on all your setbacks. That is not to say I am not human, but as time passed and I figured out complaining did not work well for me, I chose to stop doing it. It seemed like a waste of good energy, and I started to take a moment to think and breathe before reacting to things. Of course, that could sometimes be quite the challenge, but with every opportunity, I had to practice this, I had a chance to prove to myself how much I had grown. So, I choose to do just that and firmly hold my faith; the more I do it, the stronger my relationship grows in God!

I choose to share more experiences of joy with everyone I meet and to remind them that no one deserves to live in constant fear or worry all the time. If we would take a moment to think about our lives, to breathe in and weigh the situation - problems seem to become much less worrisome, and resolutions start appearing. Pretty soon, we are looking at what seemed like a bleak experience as a blessed journey. With that contagious attitude of positivity, we will begin to encounter more like-minded souls who also love to sing the Lord's praises as they move through life, living and doing His work! God has always been present with me, and like all things, He had all the people lined up to ensure that I would be properly cared for during the many different chapters of my life.

God's constant love and watching over me in life is what allowed me to grow into the person I am now, and I am hopeful that by reading through my story, you will see that I faced many things that a lot of people would judge you and throw away the key for. But, despite my sins, I was able to find the love of God and His forgiveness and live a life that provided me with an understanding that some things are out of our control and can't be changed. However, God IS in control and has a plan for all of His children. That includes each and every one of you who happens to pick up and read my book.

So, it's time for me to share my testimony with the world so that others can experience the hope I found in Christ Jesus. Remember, the very last words that our Savior left us with were hope, faith, and love, and in the Bible, we are repeatedly reminded that the greatest of those three things is and always will be *love.*

EARLIER YEARS

―――

"Before I formed thee in the belly I knew thee; and before thou camest forth out of the womb I sanctified thee, and I ordained thee a prophet unto the nations."

~ JEREMIAH 1:5, KJV

was born in Alexandria, Virginia, in the year 1980. On August 29th, my mother, Sylvia Strange, had to drive herself to the Alexandria Hospital emergency room because my father was nowhere to be found. As it turned out, my father was with his girlfriend. And as my mother found herself speeding to the hospital, it so happened that a police officer followed behind her, trying to get her to pull over, and followed her all the way to the emergency room.

She recalls that when the police officer saw her holding her stomach, he said nothing as the nurses came out with a wheelchair. She told them, "Somebody is gonna have to move it [my car] because I can't, I'm having a baby." The car was a 1969 green four-speed Roadrunner and a stick shift.

I came into the world through natural childbirth, weighing in at six pounds and three ounces, and was born promptly at 11:15 AM on a Friday. My mom's best friend, Jackie, noticed they were trying to take my rectal temperature and that it was causing me a lot of distress because I was born without one, and I was suddenly turning blue. It seemed Jackie was watching over me while my mother was having tubal ligation surgery. At this point, the medical staff also discovered something was going on with my heart. At that time, they did not know the extent of the issue, but they told my mom that I would need to be sent to another hospital, the Children's Hospital in DC or another hospital in Richmond. When given this choice, my mother chose the Children's Hospital in DC.

As a tiny infant, I was airlifted for the first time and sent to Washington, DC, while my mother drove to meet me there. The doctors spent a long time working on me in the NICU and discovered that my heart only had two chambers; usually, a heart has four chambers. Additionally, my heart had holes in and around it, a condition called Tetralogy of Fallot. This defect causes poor oxygen flow to the blood from out of the heart, and then that same oxygen-depleted blood flows into the rest of the body. The risk factors associated with Tetralogy of Fallot can be caused by a viral illness during pregnancy and a genetic history in one's family. Some associated symptoms include having blue-tinged skin and often very shallow breathing. Most patients require surgery within the first year of their life and ongoing care through adulthood.

I, however, was not just born with this defect. In addition, I was also born without a rectum, which forced all my waste to come out of my body through my vagina. The doctors thought I might have to have a sack for the duration of my life, and my mom had to learn to use small metal tools and instruments to control the flow of waste leaving my body through my vagina.

After about six months, I underwent reconstructive surgery to build my rectum. This was the second surgery I had ever undergone, but it would be the second of many more to come. My second surgery occurred when doctors used a vein from my arm to connect to my heart, improving the blood flow to my heart muscle. I will never forget having to take one too many medications for various reasons throughout my early life. I vividly remember a green medicine that tasted like pure salt, which was used to replenish my sodium intake.

As I was saying, I was born in Alexandria, Virginia, but I remember living in Delray. Living in Delray was one of the best times I can remember. Right on Commonwealth Avenue, I met my best friend, Michelle. Michelle and I did everything together. She has two brothers named Mike and Guy; we call her mom "Mema," and her dad we called "Pops." Little did I know Michelle would be my lifelong best friend and sister that I can still depend on.

This family stood by me through both good and bad times. Reflecting on my younger days, around age twelve or thirteen, I always remember sledding with Michelle, Mike, Guy, June June, Sharon, and Chris at the Masonic Temple. We slid down this long hill over and over again. We had so much fun that we almost slid into the street. Over time I had five pets: a dog, a lizard, a fish, a hamster, and a cat named Mr. Duke Strange the third. Michelle and I spent a lot of time together. One day we went to our friend Kelly's house. I was thirsty, and Kelly gave me some ice water. I accidentally swallowed a piece of ice, and I started choking. They thought I was playing at first, but then they came to help me. The guys loved to play baseball, and Michelle and I would always ask if we could play, but the answer was always no. However, they would always ask us to get the fly balls so they could continue playing.

To get money, my brother June June, Mike, Guy, and I would paint fences. Most children living in our complex went to

Mount Vernon Elementary School. We would all walk to school together. Some of my neighborhood friends were Chrystal, Dashawn, and Ronnie. It brings me joy to reflect on my earlier memories of fun, family, and hope for the future. Lord, I thank You for these fond thoughts of love and friendship.

T.C. WILLIAMS MEMORIES: HOME OF THE TITANS

"Behold the fowls of the air: for they sow not, neither do they reap, nor gather into barns; yet your heavenly Father feedeth them. Are ye not much better than they?"

~ MATTHEW 6:26, KJV

attended T.C. Williams High School in Alexandria, Virginia. Home of the Titans! T.C. Williams has a rich history and was recently re-named Alexandria City High School in July 2021. The story of Alexandria's struggle to desegregate its schools is depicted in the Disney movie, "Remember the Titans" (2000), about the high school football team who went on to win the state football championship in 1971. I remember three teachers during my time at T.C. Williams. I had a math teacher whose elevator did not go all the way to the top, an English teacher named Mr. Bullock, and Sgt., my ROTC teacher.

My Auntie Sandra lived in Maryland, and I would visit her every now and again. She had three children named Marquis, Donte, and Dwayne. She also had a foster daughter named Shavonna. Shavonna was a friend of mine. When I was about sixteen, I had a boyfriend named Dietmar. I met him while I was on the way to the mall. One day, while we were on the way to the mall, we were passing Dietmar's house, and a kid started messing with Shavonna and calling her names. She got tired of it, and she slapped him in the face. We continued our walk to the mall, even after that. Another time I cut school to meet Dietmar at the mall. He took me to Ruby Tuesday and the movies. We even tried to have sex, but it did not happen. He would even go to church with me sometimes.

Whenever things weren't going well at home, I would go to my Auntie Sandra's house. Her house was my safe space because at my house, my mother's husband (my stepfather), Charles, would yell/curse and sexually abuse me. Let's talk about the sexual abuse. Charles would kiss me on the couch in the living room and hunch. I remember him telling me, "Do not say noth-ing," or threatening something would happen to my mom.

The pain of sexual assault and abuse is something that I know a lot of young women deal with, and from my already diffi-cult upbringing, you can imagine that it caused me an equal amount of shame and pain. My fear of what other people would say and how my mother might be harmed kept me quiet for a very long time. Later, I felt incredible guilt for not stopping it sooner. Still, in the frame of mind I was in at this time in my life, I was not quite sure how to put a full stop to my nightmare, and it felt easier to go along with my abuse because I did not think anyone would believe my stepfather was capa-ble of what he was doing to me. It became easier to ignore and brush it aside, but the longer I did that, the worse I felt, and it eventually became an unbearable truth that I had to tell. While my mom was hospitalized for a hysterectomy, I felt alone, sad, and scared. I decided to go into the room with Charles, and I lay in the bed beside him for comfort, hoping that he would give me the kind of support a father should.

Suddenly, I felt his private part brush up against me, and I immediately got up and left the room. Looking back, I truly believe that if I had not gotten up, he would have tried to have sex with me. I believe that the first time this occurred, I was around twelve or thirteen years of age, but I cannot recall for sure. I will admit that there were a few occasions where I dis-missed Charles touching me and didn't put forth any effort to stop him, and I call those moments hunching. I know now that I didn't recognize what he was doing as being bad, and

I went along with it, but when I got older, I began to feel like something just wasn't right. I even remember when my step-father purchased me a diamond ring, and I think he did it as a hush gift to keep me quiet. Charles had gotten really upset about me spending more and more time with boys or even just being out of the house.

I recall visiting back home from JCS during a break. This is when I remember it being the end of his abuse. My mom was in the kitchen, my brothers were playing nearby, and then they left. My mom recalls that she heard the front door slam, and the sound shocked her to the point where she came into the living room asking, "What the hell happened?" Charles replied to her and said, "I may have touched her inappropriately." My mom came to find me outside and told me that Charles said he may have touched me inappropriately. My mom defended him and said, "He didn't mean it, Christal." And I said, "He knew exactly what he was doing." We all returned inside, and I was so upset that I walked on top of my mother's glass table to get a knife. My mother screamed at me to stop and said he wasn't worth it. Charles started saying that he didn't do anything. This only angered me even more, and I started yelling, "You knew exactly what you were doing!" Charles left then, and my brothers followed him, but he got into his truck and took off, and my brothers decided to take me with them to their house.

Shortly after that, Charles moved out, and my mom's divorce became final on July 31st. It was the quickest divorce procedure in the state of Virginia. There was one time I remember when my brothers and I were at the house with Charles, and Sydni and his girlfriend were in his room. For some reason, Charles thought they were doing something, and he began to yell and curse my brother out. Feeling accused, Sydni tried to explain himself to Charles, but he would not hear him out, and the argument got worse. June-June tried to diffuse their fighting, but Charles was belligerent and continued to yell and curse throughout the house. At that point, Ju-June had decided that was enough, and he picked up the Kirby vacuum and threw it down the stairs hitting Charles in the process. By this point, everyone decided to leave; my brothers went to their friend's house, and Sydni's girlfriend took me to church so I could be with my mom. It seemed, however, that by the time we arrived at the church, Charles had already beaten us there. When I spotted his truck in the parking lot, I knew I did not want to be there, and I asked Sydni's girlfriend to take me to Michelle's house instead. Later that evening, my mother picked me up from Michelle's house and took me to my Aunt Sandra's place. I stayed there for a couple of days and spent my time playing with Barbies, watching TV, and dancing to Aaliyah videos with Shavonna. Shavonna was the first one I told about the sexual abuse, and I felt like I could trust her since Shavonna and I had great times together. We would cook crab legs and play in the backyard, and sometimes we would walk to the mall just to have something to do. I remember having a crush on her next-door neighbor, and I would even stuff my shirt with tissue to make it look like I had boobs, hoping it would gain his attention.

I joined ROTC, and we would practice drills every day after school. There, I learned how to spin a rifle, and we competed against other drill teams. We competed in many states and won most of them. Our ROTC group went to Disney in Florida and marched in the holiday parade in Alexandria. I used to skip classes with my ROTC buddies, but we would still make it back in time for practice. Sometimes we would go to Nita's house and have pizza. They were my second family, and we even ate meals together. I became close with Sherry in ROTC. I would bring her McDonalds for breakfast; we did a lot together. We bonded over our sexual abuse experiences. Sgt. was hard on all of us because he required excellence, and we needed discipline. Although he was tough, he shaped us into a strong group of young people with respect.

Mr. Bullock organized an end-of-the-year senior trip to Paris and London. My mother gave me a choice to go on the senior trip or a brand new Volkswagen as a graduation gift. I chose to travel abroad. Although I had a great time, the trip overseas was very long and tiresome. We had a variety of students who went including a male student who considered himself female. Paris was not too friendly to people of different persuasions, colors, and gender identities. I remember one night, as we were going out to party, some locals physically attacked our diverse group. One of the funniest things that happened was that I was looking for a Fourth of July celebration. Surprisingly, I was reminded that Independence Day is celebrated in the USA, not Paris. *Dang! I forgot my history.*

Senior year was good, and I am grateful that the Lord allowed me to experience so many great things, including traveling to another country. My high school graduation was a major milestone in my life. It marked the completion of a chapter filled with tears, laughter, friendship, hard lessons, and, most importantly - growth.

The start of my life was definitely not an easy one. Still, the pattern of consistency that seemed to arise the most for me was one that constantly reminded me of the instilment of faith that had been given to me in childhood. Despite going through a terrible ordeal when my stepfather began to abuse me sexually, I found a way to keep finding a purpose in my life. I still can't fully explain what it was within me that drove me to decide to keep going because back then, I had so much anger that the idea of ever letting go of it seemed impossible.

The weight of pain from my abuse was terrible, but the idea that other people did not understand why I felt the way I did made it worse. In the years since, I've realized there is a lot of truth about being heard regarding abuse. Something happened inside me when I finally felt my voice was heard. Telling the truth now is not so much because I want people to know about it but because I want them to find the same strength and peace of mind that I found by choosing to forgive my abuser. There was a sense of power restored to me when I no longer lived in fear of being harmed by this person. When I was able to step forward and recognize that I was finally safe, I actually began to heal from the things that seemed to hold me captive to depression, misery, and sadness. I was finally set free.

I've realized that I was not the only one to endure every trial I've gone through, even as difficult as they might have been, and I now know that they are an inevitable aspect of life that comes into all of our worlds somehow or another. Sometimes it is no fault of our own, and other times we are the creators of our self-destruction. I have been both of those things, and to share my testimony with others is both a blessing and a reward because there were many times I did not know if I would live to celebrate another year, another birthday with my children, or even experience half of the beautiful things I have. It reminds me of Matthew 7:24-27, which states that a man who follows the ways of the Lord and builds a stable foundation on a rock is wise. However, a man who dismisses the sayings of the Lord and builds his foundation on sand is foolish. Do not be the latter.

I enjoyed attending and serving at Greater New Foundation Church. My Uncle Roc was the pastor, and Uncle Tom was the assistant pastor. My mom was the church clerk and also delivered the morning announcements. Mom would try her best just to give the announcements, but sometimes she would deliver a word to the congregation. This would generally add to the length of service that day. I was an usher under the direction of Mrs. Lee. I was also in the choir and went to Vacation Bible School with Shavonna.

This one Sunday, someone was chewing gum, and Donte went right over with a tissue and asked them to spit it out. Sometimes after service, Auntie Sandra and her husband, Uncle Tom, would take us to Burger King. Auntie Sandra worked for the FBI, and Uncle Tom worked for the metro bus in Virginia. One time we visited another church where Uncle Roc was supposed to preach. The spirit was high that morning, and during praise and worship, the spirit jumped on us one by one. We were so loud praising God that we were escorted out of the church. We continued to praise God in the breezeway and into the parking lot. Uncle Roc never preached at that service. Having a loving, family-oriented church that loves Christ wholeheartedly is such a blessing. Auntie Sandra put me, Shavonna, Donte, Marquis, and Dewayne together in a group called, Soldiers for the Lord. We would recite chants about being soldiers for Christ. She would say, "What are we?" And we would reply, "We are soldiers for the Lord!" I am sure many people who have read the Bible know that God says that everything has its season, and I believe mine was for just a time such as this! There is no doubt in my mind that the devil wanted to keep me beaten down, and boy, he tried.

Occasionally, I still experience something that reminds me of pain, and when thinking about sickness, I admit I can get a little intimidated. However, I can rest with God's peace around me. This has helped me to keep from becoming overly anxious. As stated above, I am a Soldier for the Lord, and as I trust Him, I will continue to praise Him for His goodness.

JOHNSON C. SMITH UNIVERSITY

"If the world hate you, ye know that it hated me before it hated you. If ye were of the world, the world would love his own: but because ye are not of the world, but I have chosen you out of the world, therefore the world hateth you. Remember the word that I said unto you, The servant is not greater than his lord. If they have persecuted me, they will also persecute you; if they have kept my saying, they will keep yours also."

~ JOHN 15:18-20, KJV

While at JCSU, I made friends with my roommate and four other girls that lived on the same floor as us. We did a lot together, which included partying. One time I made cream of chicken with rice, which became one of our go-to meals whenever the cafe was closed. A few of us enjoyed listening to go-go music. Although some people did not care for it, we did not care because we loved it. There were a lot of people from DC and Virginia at JCSU. It seemed like the other people did not like us or like our style. One night, fights erupted while a go-go band played at a gym party. Things got so out of hand that the guards shut the school down for the rest of the evening; nobody could come in or go out.

At this moment, I had to pause to reflect and think about what God would have me do. I admit that was not easy, and keeping myself from becoming anxious was one of the most difficult challenges, but this was a defining moment, and I steadied myself, took a deep breath, and kept the faith that God would keep me safe. Somehow, God kept me calm and made me realize that no matter what happened, I would be okay.

I remember a road trip we took to Myrtle Beach in three different cars. My brothers, Augusta, Guy, and Chris, were in the first car videotaping the trip. Chrissy, Mike, and Sharon were in the second car, and Michelle and I were in the third car. While driving, a guy hit the car I was in. It was happening so fast that all I could do was call out, "Jesus!" We were scared and stopped on the side of the road to check on one another. The driver pulled alongside us and said, "Go to the rest stop, use the bathroom, and you'll be fine."

When we finally made it to Myrtle Beach, we stayed in different places, but Michelle and I stayed together. When we were ready to meet up for dinner, Chrissy made everyone late because she was doing her hair and picking out her clothes. We ate at a smoky fast-food restaurant before going to the club. My other brother, Sydni, met us at the restaurant, and when we left, he accidentally backed into a pole. We all laughed at the situation. We went to the club and had a great time dancing. A guy tried to hit on Sharon while in the club, but she wasn't interested. When we left the club, the guy and Sharon began to argue over why she was not interested in talking to him. Mike went over to make sure she was okay, and then the guy and Mike began to argue. Thank goodness the argument ended calmly. My brother June June was the DJ at a club. We loved when June June played. One time when the whole gang was there, Mike, Guy, Sharon, Michelle, and I, he played "Country Grammar" by Nelly, and we all went crazy dancing.

While at JCSU, I remember one afternoon when my mother called me to inform me that she was divorcing Charles. I was happy to hear this, but she never provided any further details. Something about this news, however, gave me the courage to tell her what Charles had been doing to me. Something in her voice prompted me to tell her about the sexual abuse, and I finally felt safe enough to let my mother know what had been happening. I guess it must have been from the relief of knowing he was no longer in my immediate life or surroundings.

There was one time that I had a horrible nightmare about Charles. I recall hanging up on the Cross just like Jesus, and

I was in the living room. I awoke in fear and noticed what looked like black shadows at my door and then going up and down the streets. It was so scary, and even my cat began to act strange. It was one of the most terrifying dreams I've ever had. I immediately began calling out for my mother, and she prayed with me. There is nothing like the comfort of prayer.

I started dating a guy named Matt, who was controlling, and he cheated on me several times. Every time I would forgive him and take him back. Somehow I felt that was what I deserved. My self-esteem was low, and I did not know what a healthy relationship looked like, so I accepted how he treated me. One evening while driving down University Boulevard, we had a bad argument, and in the midst of it, I demanded that he let me out. He stopped the car, I got out, and he drove off. This was a time before cell phones, so I walked until I got to a hotel and called a cab. I believed that he would return, but he never did. I told the cab driver what happened, and although I didn't have any money to pay him, he graciously took me back to Johnson C. Smith. This was one of many accounts that I endured with him. Even after that, I chased him while he cheated and pursued other women. I thought that if I gave my body to him, he would choose me as I had chosen him. I was so gullible, and he was a liar. He told me that he was an undercover officer working for the FBI. I was honest with him and thought he would be honest with me too. Little did I know that tall, dark cup of coffee was a womanizer, and I was his victim. Looking back on this situation, everything he said was a lie, and that was a big lesson learned.

Through my tenure in college, I can truly say that I had a friend. Her name was Tina, and she was a fun-loving Queens girl who always protected me. The New York in her wanted to beat him up or have someone else do it. My college life was an okay experience. I grew up without my natural father, and although I knew of him, I didn't know him personally because he wasn't around. I could always rely on the love of my mother, brothers, and church family. My father was not a first or second thought; he was out of sight, out of mind. Once, my mom drove us to South Boston, Virginia, to see him. I remember him giving me five dollars, and I asked, "Is this because I'm five years old?" He just looked and me without offering an answer. I then turned to my mom and asked, "Can I say what I want to say to him?" Mom replied, "Yes, just be respectful." I looked at my father, handed him back the money, and said, "I think you need this more than I do. Mama, can we go now?" We got back in the car and drove home to Alexandria. I realized in my adult life that the lack of a relationship with my father left a void in me that looked elsewhere to be filled. I believe it caused me to choose mates that were not right for me and tolerated the unacceptable behaviors they displayed toward me.

All of my experiences through life have forced me to depend on God, and He took them and helped bring me out of them so that I would become more trusting in Him and find security in the miracles and works that God consistently provided me with.

As I sit back now and think about it with the fullness of truth as an adult, I know that most of the things that happened in my life occurred because I was going against the plan God had in store for me. Most of the bad places I wound up in were places God did not want me to be in, but I know some of the things that happened to me were because God wanted to keep me close to Him. I am certain that is why I faced so many barriers and had struggle after struggle thrown in my path. I now believe God planted me in some places to teach me and in others to remind me that He had a better plan all along.

After a while, I eventually left JCS, and I never finished. Tina and I were fortunate, and we got our first place together with my mom's help. Soon enough, we started working at the Residence Inn Hotel. It was a neat job, and we worked as front desk attendants. One day we were lucky enough to meet the Panthers football team while working there. The team stayed at our hotel, which was close to the stadium. Eventually, I left that location and moved to work at another location that happened to be closer to my house. The ACN Company hosted an event at our hotel, and that's where I was recruited. I spent about a year working for Residence Inn before I moved on to work at ACN. It was while working there that I met my second child's father.

"For I know the thoughts that I think toward you, saith the Lord, thoughts of peace, and not of evil, to give you an expected end."
~ Jeremiah 29:11, KJV

At one point, I had my own apartment and was still dating Matt. I was depressed, and I thought about committing suicide by taking pills. I used to work at two group homes; one was named Elon. I loved being there so much. I would help the girls and boys with whatever they needed, including doing their hair, taking them to church, school, etc. On one side were the high school kids, and the younger ones on the other. We would have activities like singing and going to the park. Courtney once sang "And I Am Telling You," from *Dreamgirls*. She did a great job. We would even go out for pizza sometimes. Two of the kids got into it while we were at the pizza shop, and we had to leave. Although the children had their moments, we always worked through them.

I became a foster parent to several children. I had a white girl named Ann Marie who wore a helmet and loved soul food, two teens (one of which had a baby), Jeremiah, Nevaeh, their little brother, Jamise and Abigail. To this day, Abigail and I keep in touch; we even share the same birthday.

As I write this, I feel compelled to let everyone know how God has been gracious to me and that I am confident He has kept His hand on me for the entirety of my life. I've always held my faith in Him and chose to cling to the Word from an early age. Proverbs 22:6 says, "Train up a child in the way he should go: and when he is old, he will not depart from it." I know that attending church and being a part of the youth choir helped shape my life and bring me back to the goodness of the Lord. From the moment I was created, just as the Bible tells us, God made me a stronger person, and even when I was brought through troubling times and the devil did his utmost to distract me from my life path, God still kept His hand firmly around me. All it takes is a reminder to trust in God, and letting go of our fears becomes a lot easier, but I did not know that until I was tested. It was only through my tests that I could see that I had the power to make a difference despite what was thrown my way.

I know now that the devil did everything he could to prevent me from being born. Being born with the disabilities I had was yet another challenge meant to force me to question God's love, which I am so grateful never won over on me. It is true that the devil looks for whom he can devour and that if it were not for God's amazing love and merciful grace, I most certainly would have been gobbled up.

Remembering that we are not the sum of our past is vital. There is hope for any person who feels burdened by the pain of your abusive past! God wants you and I to be free, which is why He made a way to redeem us from the chains put upon us by this world, all because He loves us! And it's so very simple to do. Just knowing that you can rely on Jesus makes all the difference in the world, and the only thing you need to do is let go and release your fears and allow Him to be a part of your life. I promise you, just like me, you will begin to feel and see the difference that having Him there by your side can make!

"And be ye kind one to another, tenderhearted, forgiving one another, even as God for Christ's sake hath forgiven you."
~ Ephesians 4:32, KJV

CHILDREN

"But Jesus said, 'Suffer little children, and forbid them not, to come unto me: for of such is the kingdom of heaven.'"

~ MATTHEW 19:14, KJV

God has given us free will to make our own choices in life, and I was determined to have children. I've learned that doctors are necessary and helpful, but I can not believe everything said to me, or I might never have had one but two children. If I had taken the advice of those who felt it best for me never to reproduce, I would have missed out on the beautiful opportunity to spend time with my precious children and develop such beautiful memories.

There was a period in my life when I chose to live my life as a homosexual. At that point in my life, I became involved with a woman named Amanda, and I desperately wanted a baby. After talking to my girlfriend, Amanda, I decided to ask a male friend of hers if he would be willing to donate his sperm to us so that we could be parents. He said yes, and one day my girlfriend injected his sperm into me with a turkey baster, and that was how I became pregnant with my first child.

On the day Madison was born, my mother was the very first person to hold her while I remained in recovery. While recuperating, I recall prophesying to the nurse and my brother, Augusta. The memories during that time made me question what I was doing, and having a child reminded me of the importance of having God in my life. I had been blessed with a baby and life, and I knew I needed to take better care of myself to be there for my daughter. God had answered my prayer to be a mother, and now I had more reason to keep trying in life and to try harder. I enjoyed spending time with Madison when she was younger quite a bit, to the point she went everywhere with me. We spent mommy and daughter time together in the park and doing arts and crafts. We even loved to watch Madea movies together. I looked forward to ending my day at ACN and starting my time with Madison when I got home from work. Even today, at the age of eleven, we still paint together and play games together. Madison loves to cook and serve our meals. When she gets scared, she will join me in bed for comfort. On Sunday mornings, we eat breakfast together, and each of us says a Bible verse, and then my mom comes out to close out in corporate prayer. These times we spend together are priceless, and they set a foundation for a blessed home.

While pregnant with my second daughter, Yi'Anna, my mom said it appeared that I was having a heart attack while we were going to a prenatal appointment. She pulled the car over to call 911, and we waited for the EMS to arrive. When we arrived at the hospital, they were afraid to deliver the baby because my blood pressure would not stabilize. My mother was up for the last 24 hours and was exhausted. My mom called my daughter's father to come to the hospital because she needed to go home and change clothes. She asked him to call her if the baby came while she was gone. Ty called my mother to see if Yanni had been born yet. They decided to meet at the hospital. I expired on the table during Yanni's birth and was brought back to life. Ironically, my doctor told me before my first child Madison that I couldn't have children. Then after Madison was born, it was strongly suggested that I not have another.

When mom and Ty arrived, they saw my daughter's father lying in my hospital bed, holding our newborn. My mom asked him where I was, and he said, "Don't shoot the messenger, but she can't have any visitors." My mom didn't care and left to find me, although he tried to discourage her from seeing me. Of course, that didn't sit well with my mother, so she located my whereabouts. One of the nurses told her that "my husband" requested that I not have visitors. My mom and Ty went through the roof as they set the record straight. I was not married, and the only person with authority to make any decisions about my care was my mother. Mom and Ty found me in a special area of the hospital for new heart patients. During this process, Yanni's dad was blowing up Ty's phone, trying to get us back to the room to get Madison. He had already sent Yanni back to the nursery. He was livid and complaining about being tired. When she entered the room, I asked, "Ma, where were you?" She said, "I'm here now," and requested that my baby be brought to me. I was relieved to see her, and when I saw Yanni, my blood pressure regulated. I had to stay at the hospital for about a week before being discharged home. My mom offered us to stay with her, but I declined because Yanni's dad and I were living together. We struggled financially to the point that when I returned home after delivery, our water was cut off, and there was no place for the baby to sleep, although he promised there would be. I went to stay with my mom for a day, but I took care of the water situation and returned home. Motherhood was fine for the most part; however, my relationship was breaking down. He would be upset that I would spend much time with my children, not him. I even wanted to pursue painting and other business ventures, but he turned them down and always responded, "Not now."

I have realized through the things I have experienced in life that there is a way to survive and thrive in a healthy life, but it requires that we cease to be preoccupied with ourselves and begin to focus on the God-given way the Bible recommends. Once we begin doing this, it becomes a lot easier to do the introspection: to look within ourselves and reflect on our choices and who we want to be. It becomes so easy to become absorbed with our welfare and to feel sorry for ourselves when we are victimized; however, keeping a victim mentality is a disservice to ourselves, and I had to learn this the hard way. I had a lot of scars, both physical and spiritual.

I also had emotional and mental injuries that had not yet been healed, and I needed to find a way to fix myself. I found that the only way to do that was to turn back to God, but not partially, fully, completely, and wholly because our Savior gave up His life so we can be free. How could I not trust Him after being willing to do all that? As a child of God, I have grown tremendously, but you can see it was no easy thing for me to do. I had to go through several character-building moments, and I often had doubts and questioned myself. I was only seeking love, but I went about it the wrong way at times, and the devil wanted me to believe I did not deserve it. The devil wanted me to believe that God didn't love me and that I was unworthy of being loved, but I came to learn that was not the case, and I thank God daily for His unending and all-encompassing love. Our Father in heaven is a merciful and loving God, and all He asks is that we trust in Him; turn back to him, repent of our sins, and step into the life He intended for us to have.

I started to open myself up for love again but ended up with my heart broken again. I thought I had been heartbroken before, but this time it felt different. The only thing he gave me was an "I'm sorry." I truly did love this man, but my heart will heal in time. As I follow Christ, I will follow His Word, which includes no sex before marriage. It became important to me to follow God's plan for me and stay steadfast in holding to the commitment to my abstinence. I figured if a man had a heart after God, he would desire to do what God hoped for us and do things properly. Now that I opted to do things in a much more biblical way, it did not seem like that much of a loss to me because any man who pressured me or went against that would be going against the plans God had set in motion for me. It was a test to see whether we were meant to be, and I decided that not allowing my heart to be wickedly deceitful was in the best interest of myself, my children, and my relationship with God.

SURGERY AND RECOVERY

"Is any sick among you? let him call for the elders of the church; and let them pray over him, anointing him with oil in the name of the Lord: And the prayer of faith shall save the sick, and the Lord shall raise him up; and if he have committed sins, they shall be forgiven him."

~ JAMES 5:14-15, KJV

was born with Tetralogy of Fallot (TOF) and have had five open-heart surgeries. TOF is an incredibly rare medical condition, and less than 20,000 births produce infants with the condition. TOF causes many issues and ailments; in my case, I was born with only two heart chambers with holes present all around them. I was not very old when this began causing me issues, and I remember experiencing my first heart attack at my grandmother's house. During this experience, my mother had to give me mouth-to-mouth while driving me to Richmond, where the paramedics airlifted me to the Children's Hospital in DC. Throughout my life, I've spent a lot of time in a hospital because of my heart condition.

My heart specialist, Dr. Green from Charlotte, referred me to Duke Hospital for surgery. Of all my doctors, he was my favorite. On the day of my fourth open-heart surgery, my girlfriend, Renee, mom, and brothers were all there with me. After the surgery, a nurse came in to give me medicine. I asked her what she was giving me, and she went off with an attitude. In the middle of the nurse ranting at me, my mother entered my hospital room and felt compelled to report the nurse, having her immediately removed from providing me any further care.

I've had many scary ordeals, including dying upon the delivery table while in labor with my second child. Fortunately, I was revived. I had to have stents put into my heart, and a month later, I had my fifth and final open heart surgery because of blood clots forming in my blood vessels. No blood or oxygen was going to my brain, and I was in and out of a coma for over a month. While in a coma, I saw my grandmother, and she said, "It is not your time."

> *"And now men see not the bright light which is in the clouds: but the wind passeth, and cleanseth them."*
> ~ *Job 37:21, KJV*

Then God asked me if I would choose to stay with Him or to go back, and I chose to come back because I still had work to do. The doctor said I would not walk or talk at all, but I'm doing it, and although the doctor said one thing, God has the final say. My mother would have gospel music playing while in my hospital room. When I came out of my coma, I sang the gospel song "There's a Bright Side Somewhere." I spent my recovery at the Brain Center. While there, a friend named Lewis always went outside with me. Tasha was my physical therapist who helped me with my left hand, using a splint to keep it open. Tammy did activities with us like exercising, make-up, games, etc.

On Halloween, she took us trick-or-treating, and on Sundays, there were two pastors that held services in the morning and afternoon. Tammy also had someone play music for us. I did have a roommate, but I also did not care for the food. My mom would bring my children to visit me. Yanni's father would also bring her to visit, but because I was afraid of him, I would sit with my back facing him when he would bring her to visit.

While at the Brain Center in recovery, my child's father tried to take me to court for child support and sole custody. Although he was not granted child support, he was given shared custody with my mom and me. My mom had to fight for visitation rights so I could see my baby. During the proceedings, my mom and brother had to speak for me, and the judge had to tell my mother to shut up. My mom was the power of attorney to speak for me because I physically couldn't. It seemed as if my whole family came to support me; we took up one whole side of the courtroom. My mom decided to take me out of the Brain Center because my feet began to curl inward, and I had to have surgery on them. I went to rehab in Charlotte, and they helped me to walk and bathe myself again within two weeks. When I was sent home, they gave me a wheelchair, and after I got home, my mother said "No," to the wheelchair and encouraged me to walk. I returned to the Brain Center to see Tasha and Tammy and showed off my walking.

"Fear thou not; for I am with thee: be not dismayed; for I am thy God: I will strengthen thee; yea, I will help thee; yea, I will uphold thee with the right hand of my righteousness."
~ Isaiah 41:10, KJV

"To every thing there is a season, and a time to every purpose under the heaven: A time to be born, and a time to die; a time to plant, and a time to pluck up that which is planted; A time to kill, and a time to heal; a time to break down, and a time to build up; A time to weep, and a time to laugh; a time to mourn, and a time to dance; A time to cast away stones, and a time to gather stones together; a time to embrace, and a time to refrain from embracing; A time to get, and a time to lose; a time to keep, and a

time to cast away; A time to rend, and a time to sew; a
time to keep silence, and a time to speak; A time to love,
and a time to hate; a time of war, and a time of peace."
~ Ecclesiastes 3:1-8, KJV

I have truly been through a lot in my lifetime, and some experiences I'll never forget. The events that happened the night before my last open heart surgery are eternally etched in my memory bank for life. Every time I think about it, I get emotional. God will have to help me through this, but I know HE IS a healer. I will give it to the Lord because only He can help me. I do not know why God let me remember these things, but I think it's because writing this book will help others. I'm taking my power back! I'm going to handle it with love like God says I should. God brought me through comas, not talking or walking, so I know He can get me through this. Through it all, I never lost my faith; He has always been in the background.

I feel compelled to let every reader who comes across this know that just because God allows tests does not mean He does not love us or does not want us to do well in life. Remembering that God wants us to pass every trial He puts before us is essential. When He allows them to come, it is to see if we have learned valuable lessons so that we can go on to our next venture in His plan for our prosperity, happiness, and overall joy.

God is a lovely Father and the Creator of all that is beautiful in the world. We must remember that by going through tests and overcoming them, we earn rewards and grow closer to Him in our walk. God wants us to pass these tests. He desires to see us overcome our trials.

God will allow us to be put before the snare so that He can teach us to rely on Him and to help us succeed on our life path, and do so with tremendous and beautiful abundance and everlasting joy and love. If we only give Him the opportunity, God will help make our dreams tangible.

I am a miracle, and I understand now I am here to show you that God is real, and still, I stand. This is why people say I'm a miracle. If you read my story and knew about me, I'm not supposed to be here. But if you are reading this, please give thanks to God. I do every day, and I hope and pray that reading my story will bring you closer to Him. He is listening; just talk to Him because He is waiting for you.

www.ingramcontent.com/pod-product-compliance
Lightning Source LLC
Chambersburg PA
CBHW051558120626
46551CB00013B/1580